Rain Grows Bows

Embracing Transformation in the Storms of Life

Mary Elizabeth Holt

BookLeaf Publishing

India | USA | UK

Dedicated to my beloved pets;

Zoey, and Twilight.

Acknowledgement

To my family—thank you for every word of encouragement. I love you all. To the advertisement on social media that provided the link to set this up: thank you. To everyone working on the project: I see your effort, and I appreciate you. And to the Canva AI that created the artwork for the cover based on a few key words: very cool stuff, I love it bunches. Thank you, Chat GPT.

Preface

For finding silver linings, and choosing to see the bright side. The collection is a journey based on daydreams, and days spent. May it illuminate a perspective on life that is optimistic in spite of difficulties.

Bow the Rain

When it's dark,
The stars will shine;
A sparkle so divine.
And as you look up at the sky,
They bring glitter to the night.
Some simple beauty, so strikingly unlike
A contrasting canvas of twilight.

So when it rains,
Instead of feeling your spirits low,
Let your gaze rise and
Focus on
Looking up
To see the bow.

Salutations

Welcome to the field of woo;
A place where all blue flowers bloom.
And if they ask "What are their hues?"
I hope they say they're of sea and sky;
My spaces two.

Salutations—it is free
A personal feat for being so flappy.
For fun, I sit and sip some tea,
Looking for blue butterflies
To remind me of the sea.

They say a butterfly that flaps its wings
Can cause a future tsunami.
They dwell in fields of flowers,
With leaves and stems of green.

Can Teen

During the day,
Of work with no play,
I'm simply feeling somber.
To pass the time,
I live within the mind—
An imaginary loner.
To watch a video
And drift into a dream
Is my favorite thing
While in the canteen.

Four Legs

What do they do
For a horse who can't see?
Does a foal with failing eyes
Get assigned
Glasses,
Or is it simply blind?
What a wonderful thing to think:
Assistance for animals with disabilities.

For example, Zoey,
Whose eyesight is fading;
Where once was brown,
It is now cloudy.
She mostly reacts to sound—
A dog that's aging.

For our companions,
Sight's so worth saving.
How would it alter
Their behavior?
Oh, how... oh, how
Could humans cater
To our forest friends that waver?

Cheesesteak Sandwich

Today is the only day
We ever have on earth.
Not worried about the past;
It doesn't exist,
And neither does the future.
I must be reminded
At the moment:
Feelings are fleeting, but so is food.
How to remember
The present is no fluke?

Within a recipe
There may be many things,
And such is life as well.
Honestly, I'm probably just hungry;

Enticed by the smell.
Time to take an early lunch,
So later I'm able to sell.

Sautéed fervor, fickle and salty.
Or is it only the onions?
Will this passion pass
After cheesesteak sandwich consumption?

(Yes indeed.)

Warm Lighting

A thud echoes into the brisk breeze,
Piercing through long sleeves.
Pavement greeting worn feet,
Now grounding after a journey.
The deep glow of a street
Reflected by mustard leaves—
Season's greetings.
Here, well after the lamps have first wakened.

Finally, turn a familiar knob.
Tiny toes click on their way,
With wagging tails
And eyes that say,
"Where have you been today?"
Since words can't be woofed,
Some whines will suffice.
Welcomed by cleaning supplies,
And fur bathed in warm lights.

Twin Clover Fly

How long does it take to find a four-leaf
clover in the field of weeds and leaves?
It depends on how lucky
And keen the clover fiend is feeling.
One might suggest settling for a feat
Such as looking for one with two leaves—
A heart mirrored back-to-back kind
Of thing.
After seeing a bi-clover, one might agree
It may just be just as lucky.
It looks like a butterfly
With two wings.
It looks as if it may fly away and find its
partner.
In fact, it doesn't seem like settling at all.

In fact, from now on, searching for a bi-clover
is a new kind of game.
See the beauty within everything.

BAD (What's Pretty)

Beauty resides within the mind.

Attributes include joy and cunning.

Destined to succeed are those

Whose battles are ever-becoming.

Physical charm may seem divine,

But who truly are they inside?

Attention gives to the outside—

Don't be fooled by sheepskin hide.

When we all age and live a life,

People end up the same with time.

Bottles may feed infanticide,

And that is just the start.

Dare to seek those with the truest heart.

Twilight Unstow

Soaring seagull, sell me the sun;
Barter halos in the sky.
Roaring blues and rolling hues run—
Oh, how I want to fly.

Whisper softly, simple bird, so
Memories can sail through here.
Cotton candy clouds drift slow,
Revealing the cosmos near.

Amber showers bring twilight;
Each sharp inhale is so finite.
Indigo is daring to show.
How is it so close without a flight?

The night is simple and divine;
The stars whisper delicately.
The white wisps spiral into time,
The rinse-off of the day's finality.

Coming of Age

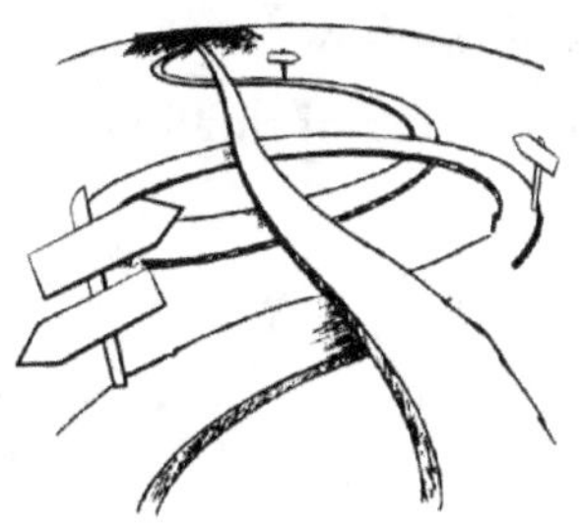

Pot of gold
At the end of the rainbow,
But commercials only last 30
Seconds or so.
Mallow Charms meant
Lime leprechaun.
Now bills grow.

A fateful fable upon
Utopia glows,
Where are we, bright bows?
Feats of victory wait for us,
Along these roads of rainbow.

Should we follow
Adult sorrows and dreary tomorrows
With happiness borrowed?

I'd still choose both.
Hope knows of rainbows;
Take blows in the era of flowing
Technicolor.
Illuminate the faintest lows.

Congregate

How often does one look up?
Maybe not enough.

If they ever take the time to focus on what's
above,
It may be love.

Most only glimpse a sliver
Of the waking world.
To deliver a bigger picture,
One must consider more.

Emotions are a ladder
That they climb each day.
Even the blind can see them
From the vantage point of hate.

One lives between both realities—
Of the ground and the birds' eye view.
When at a rising vantage point,
Others aren't so different from any people or
creatures in pursuit of food.

Perspective is a question, and can be altered
thus.
To see the world as separate is an illusion
lacking trust.
Even plants have been known to congregate
and colonize Earth's land.
Each creature, from foot to soil, could be kin
to the common man.

'Til 'Tis Did

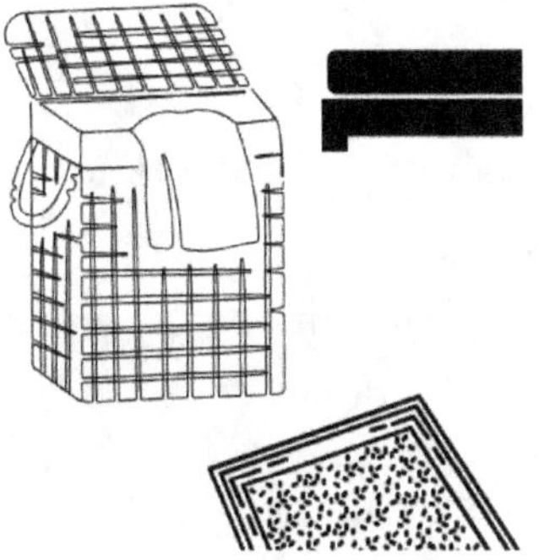

Wicker basket with a lid, now grown so heavy.
Of course, it's past due for its time to be
carried.
It used to be for weeks that linens stayed
there clean,
And made the delicate clothes so wrinkled.

Tropical paradise can only keep lingering in
fabric so long,
Scent beads seem like just another step, and
allergies can't handle too many chemicals
anyway.
It's time for them to be put away.
Nowadays, there's a routine to get it done
each week.

Consistency lessens the workload, and when
it's easy, it's more likely to be completed.

So make the chores fun.
Do it one pair of pants at a time, paused
between songs.
Do it after a snack and before a snack.
Do it not till it's done—
Just to do it is enough.

Dancing in the closet to a glittery pop
melody,
Each week, the chore of folding clothes seems
daunting until I sing.
As the basket gets lighter, dryer sheet
trophies signify the deed is done.
Now the question remains: just how can one
make dishes fun?

Read a Map

No one has ever taught me
How to read a map.
It must not be important
If I can rely on an app.
Though one day, if the world drops
Internet for sap,
I might be lost and forced to learn how to
navigate by paperback.

No one has ever taught me
How to do my taxes.
It must not be important
And there's an app for that.

Though one day, if the world goes
From internet to grass,
We may not need so much paperwork.

I never did like math.

Something I have learned,
From all these days on Earth,
Is that you must do research
On things you want to be.
Oftentimes, to be free,
You must learn alone, act alone, and see
How to be a human
In times like these.

Violets

Blue bumble   bee bait.

I crave velvet—fading fate.

True euphoria.

Adroit at Taffy

Like the sunset;
Rays of flavor.
Enough to share,
Enough to savor.

Have some now or have some later.
When peeled quickly,
What remains feels like paper.
For best results, you need the labor.

To take the time
And peel it greater
Yields bald results—
A talent scraper.

Change

Let the hyenas cackle; they fill the savannah
with their hate.
Carry on, dear one;
Step closer to your fate.
And as you taste desire,
(Bubbly like champagne)
The whines will grow louder,
But be led not by the rain.
Love is the language of success,
And only love can leave your stain.

There's this habit made by vultures
Of following the weak,
They wait for them to fall, and then
They do finally feast.

Some may be like vultures,
And when they sense you're meek,
They flutter, pick, and prance about,
Waiting for some meat.

If there's a school of fish
Swimming steadily upstream,
A reason to go against the current
(A feat not done with ease,)
Not to follow the herd of sheep
Undoubtedly means something.

Let it be a lesson that persistence can prevail.
What was once a single choice
To challenge a system frail
May be a school of change someday.
To find your way,
You may have to not be the same.

Adaptable

To put in a nail—it's aggressive.

A hammer is

Perfectly suited.

A hammer is not as useful

When trying to screw in a screw.

Both the front side and the backside

Simply cannot so delicately do

What it takes to screw in a screw.

One may be able to improvise.

For a hammer, sometimes, I use a soup can.

Always something strong, but what it is

Depends on how deep it needs to go,

And how thick the wall,

And how thin the nail.

A toolbox is equipped

With a hammer and other tools.

You simply need to know

The most useful one to use.

Sometime I improvise—

For a screwdriver, I might

Use a Phillips head instead.

Turn it on its side,

Or even a butter knife.

Oftentimes, one needs a hammer

For something like a nail.

But when confronted with a screw
you need another tool to prevail.

And Nothing

Hi, my name is Mary.
Do you know me?
Nobody does know me; they only know what
they assume they see.
That's the problem; things aren't as they seem.
What you see is what you get?
But you don't always get what you see.
Sometimes, you don't like what you get.
Sometimes, you crave what you see.

Well, here's a newsflash from me:
I'm not what I seem.
I'm dark and mean.
I'm nice and sweet.
I'm everything—
And also nothing.

Problems Tree

People run from problems,
Why?
Problems make you good.
The challenges they face each day
Reinforce our wood.

Issues we once saw as towering then
Slowly shrink away.
By the end, what once was meant
To saw us down may even stay.

There's this thing inside the brain
That defaults to comfortable.
It fights change at any cost;
It takes away your growth.

If you take to water, you can increase its flow.

If you choose to stay the same,
Just know it's had its way.
Because it's easy to just be
And find a thing to blame.

So why try?
Why work to be more
When it's causing you to be so sore?
What is all this growing for
But needing a new pot for more roots
And extra leaves to prune?

Well, it's more of you.
More of me?
Growth is a celebration—to look back and see
how far we came.

That without blame or shame, we did all this
Even though it wasn't easy or seemed
impossible.
It was done, and it may be more doable next
time.

Why whine about feats defeated?
Hoops jumped through?
You were true.
You did you.

Sweep a Street

Wind whipping and branches torn,
When dusk's darkness overtook the day,
And monsoon rain
Coated the Earth with debris,
It was some time before the streets were
clean.
Most waited for the trucks to come
To clear the twigs and leaves.
One young woman decided to sweep her
street,
Armed with a broom and a bottle of water.
In a couple of hours, she was able to get her
car to a main road from home..

In the night, heat receded.
She took to the street
And kept on sweeping.
Thanks to her determination, they were able
to get to the gas station.
By week's end, the street was cleared of
debris, just as the street sweeper trucks
showed up.

For two weeks, there was no power.
Potatoes baked in aluminum foil under the
fire,
Smelling like ashes;
Tasting of smoky sides.
Neighbors shared packaged beef stew that
was microwaved by a car-to-wall plug adapter
and some gasoline.

If it's one against the hurricane, they surely
will lose,
Unless we all grab a broom;
It's your street, too.
If a project is too big, we all hold hands
'Til tis' did.

Feats of Feeding

First in the row is an apple tree—
Essential food to keep us free.
Next I'd try the clementine,
And plant some neatly in a line.
Wouldn't you know, lemon is another row;
That makes three.
For health's sake, let's add avocado.
A dream garden, and not just for show—
To make a place for
Blueberries to grow.
One more thing before the yard is complete:
A vine of grapes on which to feast.

Other things to include in this recipe:
Tomato, potato, and cabbage please.

Imagine if we all grew our own veggies?

Of course, I could trade red apples for green,
And my next-door neighbor could pick from
my trees.

If we all had some, what else would we need?

A meticulous lawn is a beautiful thing,
But it doesn't seem so practical
In a world where we all eat.

And the image of a rainbow garden seems like
a beautiful thing.
Though grass is a nice lawn, (all trimmed and
clean)
Maybe it isn't the most practical
In a world where we all eat.

Breathe Underwater

Come up, age of gamers,
Where we can see the quest.
How do you pass this test?
Is there a glowing halo,
Or maybe a yellow question mark?
The game of life is so very fun.
It appears that games are everywhere,
And we're all caught up in one.
Choose your place to live, the car you drive,
and the job you have;
The game where we spend all of our time.
But what if you're more of a reader,
And instead of games, you hide?
What if you'd rather be grounded. soaking in
a bubble bath than play?

What if you'd rather write?
For sure, playthroughs have their place,
But can't we live in a space
Where we can all go at our own pace?
Such modern technology surely could
accommodate
For those who find themselves in last place.
When you judge a fish by its ability to climb a
tree,
You may praise
The monkey,
And never see the value in being able to
breathe beneath the sea.

Cliche

In the end,
They first were friends—
When quarrels cast shame.
Over time we valentines
Play anime and games.
Unity brings lights to these
Nights of original memories.

Through thick and thin,
We are a team—
We conquer all our enemies.
Future reveals no tales or deeds,
For lovers echo destiny.

In the depths of my despair,
I saw a lock of hopeful hair.
Its strands called out to set me free—
Unbound by logic'c' pull on gravity.

Oh if they saw what I did see—
Eyes of aqua galaxies.
A world of wonder waits for me;
Where constellations speak in prophecy.

You are my other half.

Disassembled

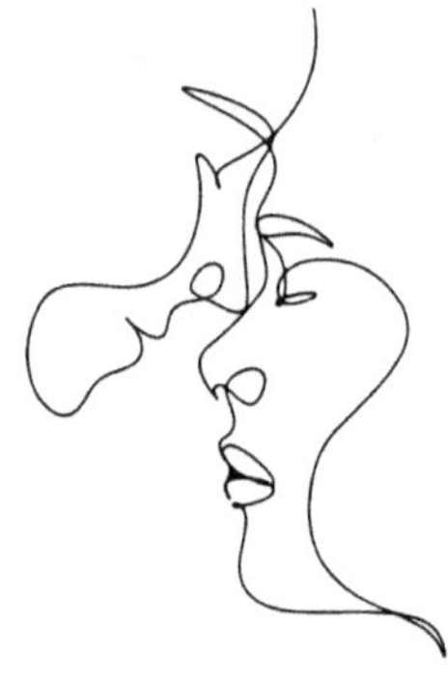

Things fall apart to come back together
The right way.
Sometimes in life it might seem
In disarray—
Like the weather is not in your favor;
Plants need rain.

When the night sky is dim,
Some stars can shine through.
Even city lights can't cover them
Once one travels into
A place so green,
To peek through trees
At Orion's belt
(depending on the geography of their scene).

Mary Christmas

Meticulous particulars
Engulf a day of jolly.
Problematic pragmatics
Wilt our springs of holly.
The folding and holding of various things...
I want to be where the little ones see;

Amber glowing on wrapping paper,
Candy, cookies, and holiday feasts—
Melodies of cheer to accompany peace.
So simple to live and so freeing to be.
I wanna feel that imagination station,
And walk within the scene.
Younger eyes see more than me;
I want to be where the little ones flee.

You, sir, give me my reason to be.
The happiness postponed is now set free—
I cherish my loving family.
To the webs that we weave,
In you I believe;
Our future is concrete.

Are We

Are you the lesson, or the destined?
The rain, or the bow?
I'm not sure how to lessen
The questions,
And so they flow.
Are we destiny?
Is fate so fickle here?
The only thing I need to know will happen
when you're near.
I have a sense,
At your expense,
It will lend me context, no less.
I know you're dense,
But time will tell then.

We'll tell them.

Mother

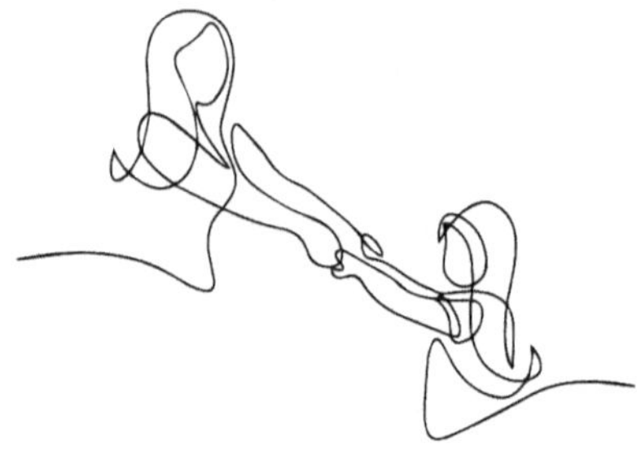

I am the nest
Where people come by to rest.
I am the shade,
A reprieve from a sunny day;
Those solemn rays
I keep at bay.

I am the tall glass of light.
I am the kite you fly when there's easy wind.
I am the breath beneath a raspy floor.
They keep me tamed,
And I abhor
These shackled chains
And asphalt core.

I am the stain;
They mark my lore.

It's not the same as they say—
I am in vain.

Though when you need a place,
I'm always open arms and
A warming heart.
Yet mine is sold.
I fall apart.
But if you ever need
A place to rest your soul,
I'll open up my doors
And help to make you whole.
Paying tolls for my role of cheering up chores.
Even when sore,
If duty calls, I'd carry you home
On my back like a pack.

Sloth

I should get up and pee (just haven't had the
energy.)
Is it lazy
To procrastinate relief?
For surely this feat
Would contribute greatly
To me.
So why do I wait
To satiate
This need?
Seeing yellow, and hearing seas.
Explain this roaring river
Being dammed up, please.

Well this cocoon is more comfortable
Than any place I'm not,
And until it overcomes that,
My need to pee means squat.

Oh how I drank that water,
With legs so keen
To get up and fill the cup.
Where are they now
That I need to pee?
Curled up and cozy,
Wanting only to sleep.

If there was ever a moment
For a motivational speech
It would be
For when it's time to rise from bed;
A place so keen.

Sprinkles

In the rising dawn,
Its air
Wisps around and drags your hair.
One step, two, and up to four,
You courageously walk past the front door.

Some time slips by, and now you're there.
The sky is coral,
And the day is fair.

A whiff of beans,
And you've seen sprinkled things
Behind the transparent wall that leans.
Its angle permits you to peer through
And select a doughed-up food.

Strawberry glaze.
Creamy taste.

What could start off better today
Then a dessert
With a decadent drink to wash it away?

Queens

She dreams of bigger things;
Of golden rings,
And woven tapestries.
A blue sky day—
Tell her you'll stay.
For fate is paradise
If they play this game.
Worth the wait
For clarity,
To know her fated date
Once the clouds wash away.
They carry peace.
Sometimes it has to fall apart
To be reassembled correctly.

Secrets to Ashes

Imagine making the most
Of a terrible situation,
Just to be told that's your fixed destination.
Conquering this place
Just proves that's what it was built for;
Labor.
No time for upgrades only time to
Sustain
This distasteful system.
Its rhythm of daily activity—
Preached as sacred wisdom
Rather than the desire
To live comfortably.
Speak empty to the fire—
It keeps your secrets dear.
Say what you think where no one will hear;

Consumption is fake,
And recycle the fear
To living in love,
Because once the rain clears
We'll have bows.

Balance

To keep with the rhythm of this music—
Physically moving
With the tune
Is
A skill divine.
Find the time
To practice dances;
It's essential for the mind to greet movement.
Body and brain are partners,
And if you see the signs,
Then follow the expectation
Of the beat you find.
Yes, there's choreography.

And instead, you can move the feet
However you would like.
It's up to you to follow suit
Or be on your own time.

Fruit Soup

Asmoothie is a soup.
When you combine and grind some things,
And then consume them
Deliberately,
The concoction is a potion
That
Leaves you fed.

Is it soup instead?
When you bake some veggies, you can grind
them too.
It would make a broth
Savory to consume.

But when combining fruits,
And a taste is laid,
It may be less savory,
But a blend is made.

Headwear

So debt is the norm?
How could they conform?
Each honors the system
In every uniform.
Every hat they adorn,
For housing to afford,
Is honoring its fallacy;
Just look for the horns.
It's a necklace—
Worth the solution to homelessness
That they abhor.
Hunger is a crisis.
If we all sit,
They can't eat it.
Karma is a chore.

Onions Have Layers

Knight in shining armor—
Ride your horse to the tower.
A hero clad in silver;
One that never cowers.

Fight the dragon.
Save the princess.
Share your valor,
One who never misses.

Metal is mostly fireproof,
And time is finite.
So sleuth out its whereabouts,
To find the loot of love.

She's waiting patiently, but doubtful.
She'll come around though.
Pacing in a tower,
Keeping to her own bounds.

Cross The Street

Hold their hand if you need to—
The young and elderly
Seek for assistance with
Steps over sidewalk
Across asphalt crosswalks.

Certain species pitter patter
O'er the blacktop during dusk.
They know no better than to trust
Drivers in the night.
Headlights—
The only guidance.
And despite
Persistence,
Some never make it to the other side.
Be diligent, dear.

Puzzled

A picture of each puzzle is on the front of the
box.
Otherwise, it would be incredibly hard to put
together.
And once it's built, one may disassemble it
Given that it's easier to store
In several pieces.
And once created, it can be marveled
At, but may be destroyed later.
Don't worry, it could always be rebuilt again,
As long as it is known—
What it looks like in the end.

Module

Our sun rises
And sets
Each day on your chest.
Hope intertwines with reality
Settling in.
We do our best,
And that's all we need.
When stress
Poses the questions
Directed at lessons—
Growth is not always comfortable.

Habits

Forest critters need to feed.
Are we allowed to feed them, please?
When humans take over Earth's geography,
Where else can they get their cranberries?
Who else could teach humanity
Better than these plethora of animal families?

Beavers?
No one builds a better dam.
Hawks?
Operational optics—we design our cameras
by.
Sharks?
Naval ships have exteriors inspired by their
skin.

Well then give back to the ones under attack
by deforestation.
Unlike
Colonization of a planet
Unclaimed
By a singular species,
When billions deserve these
Endless bounties.

Diet Soda

Truly, sweetness is laced with something.
Is sugar good for you?
Honey may be the healthier thing,
And candy
Is surely not.
But
As someone with access to all sweet things,
(And a tendency toward tastebud fulfillment)
Some indulgence is not
The worst.
Flavor first.
Ah, yes,
Fruit is nature's candy.
And sweet tea is next to nothing;
The best beverage.

Opinions are average.
Thin and minty cookies,
And whipped cream
With cherries
Are delicacies
Worth saving
For special occasions.
A small treat
For completing a task
Or a large feat—
No reason too lacking.

When trying to avoid overconsumption of
dessert rations
One may take to dieting options.
Zero soda is a go-to choice.
Might be silly to compromise...
Might be wise.
For optimizing balance
Is the best advice.

Step One

Do you sit
In a soft chair?
How often are you walking
Here and there?
Is stillness required,
And should you stay put?
What do you do daily
To feel as one should?

Some try jogging, swimming, and the like.
However you can provide the best exercise
Is yours to determine, if you choose to
comply.
The hardest part is starting—

A single step is more than nothing.
If one block is all you've got inside you, then
A battery depleted is the task completed.

So glad you've seen it through.
For each practice encourages endurance,
And sometimes tries are null.
As long as you honor perseverance,
Progress will surely show.

Cough Syrup Tastes Very Bad

I don't like going to the doctor's office—
They often poke and prod.
I don't like being examined, honestly
I'd rather just go home.

I don't want to visit the dentist today.
That feeling, it may never fade.
I don't want a numb tongue—
I'd rather feel my gums all day.

I don't like being ill that much,
And if it's just a prick,
Then maybe the visit could be worth it
If it means I'll no longer be sick.

I don't want cavities in my teeth,
So if I truly must,
I can simply sit on this cushioned bench
And try not to kick up a fuss.

There are things I do not prefer at all
That I choose to do.
And when I ask myself why,
I find the worst is over so soon.

Lulla-Bye Baby

It is time to sleep.
Goodnight.
It is time to rest.
It is the hour to say goodbye.
And when we wake, I'll be there again.

I know that night is long, my dear.
I choose to stay so late,
And would rather not let you go.
It's twilight and the moon is calling us here
To dream a sweet dream alone.

Don't fret, this is not a long split.
Oh, please don't make it tough.
I want to throw a fit too—
I want another hug.

There will come a time when you may be far,
So I just need you to know
That this goodbye,
And one each night,
Is simply a future hello.

Pristine

Yarn—either inextricably bound, or
decorative streamers.
One could barely get in the door.
For fear of entering the room—a tear.

A fan whistled,
Spitting dust about.
Invisible carpet reeked of something six feet
underground.

After a bag was filled, and then two more,
Cups were taken—
Filled with squishy, slimy, stinky, spewing
Gobs of month-old, unidentified drinks.

Cardboard socks leave a whiff with
T-shirts, shorts, and knee-length pants
All piled in a corner.

Under the bed lay a germaphobe's horrors.

Each dresser drawer held sleeves reaching out
at you,
Begging to be folded or hung up.
The towel heap grew into a musty stew.

Strown paper on the floor
Sticks to feet with a gooey residue—
A garden of wrappers orchestrating footsteps.

The childhood stuffed animals all
Flexing on the bed;

A bed pristine.

Yellow Bricks

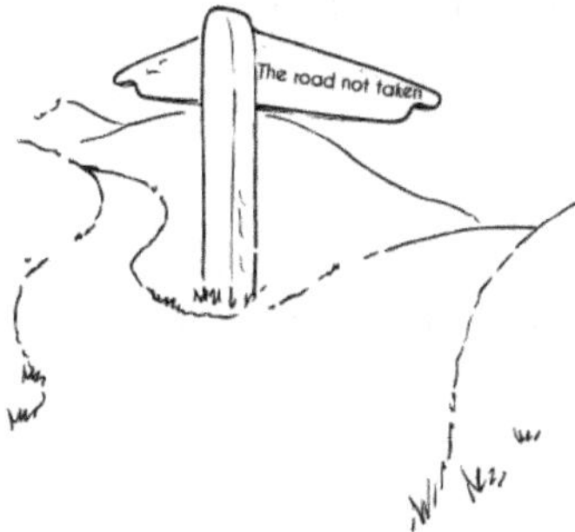

What if this is the missed opportunity?
What if bliss is simply
Opening eyes to this light inside that's been
Waiting the whole time?

What if the answers were never lost,
But still, hushed whispers
That were walking with us all along?

What if strength is knowing
When to be strong,
When to let the feeling take over,
And how to acknowledge weighted
shoulders?

What if escape is okay?

So what if it's underrated?
Perspective is a key player
In knowledge, freedom, and fate.

So what if it's late?
When paths deviate they have
Far more to compensate for.

So what if the journey is the destination?
The lesson is what you take
From it.

So what if questions are open ended,
And never get answered the same way?
Learning and growing means
Responses may
Shift.

So what if we vary when things get hairy—
Consistency is cake.

Salt

When it's dark,
Look for stars
To see a silver lining.
The light will pierce through—
Illumination's dew.
They bring unto the night,
In the diminished and dark
Twilight,
A sparkle and glory so divine.

Rainbows only raise during the day,
But wouldn't it be great
To see one
Up in the stars?
Such contrasting bars

Of fragmented light
Would happen to be bright,
(Like an LED strip)
Bestowed on this speckled sky.

Oolong

Fond of leaves
Drenched in steam,
With a splash of cream.
Familiar flavor—
Soul feed.
Stomach relieved
From its aching.
Funny how brewing,
After consuming,
Can feel so fleeting.
Drinks are complete.

Development

I am who I was,
And then some.
From all that's above,
I have become
So far in this life.
Is it mine?
I found out why
It's about time
We define
Our minds
As divine,
But they aren't aligned with logic. I find
That memories are a fallacy—
The scope of our own lenses through which
we see.

Not rational, but they are whole.
It's who we are;
The crafted parts.
Epiphanies when memories take hold.
Not contingent on success, but rooted in
happiness.
And I digress—
The fur de-stress, but then distress
About bittersweet pets,
And losing them
Compresses.

Banana Spider Brownies

Laugh in the faces of
Clowns.
When asked about
Frowns,

Don't fret.

The curious can take a smile,

So simmer with it for quite a while.

See, when teaching, you must show
humility—

For learning is a capability.

Tour Bus

On the Fourth of July
Is when the eagles fly.
There is so much to ogle at
In these modern times.
To travel today
Around the USA
Should be sublime.

How many cafes,
Ketchup laden
Buns,
And french fries
Could be toured?

Not even mentioning the rest of the world.
It'll start here, and then spread out.

Adventures are the best things to write about.

Parallel

In my dreams, I can fly.
I can move objects with my mind.
I can see through time,
And walk through walls.
In that realm, I have it all.

In a world that we create,
What would and should exist?
There is no place for strife in a meditative
state,
Nor burdens to enlist.

When I wake, it is in a place that I dearly
miss.

What a world to live in—

A transcendence.

Zoey Blue Holt

I love my dog
Like a dear.
She sings a song
When I draw near.
Although a whine
Is not in rhyme,
She says it loud and clear;

"I love it when you're here."

And in the days
Where we are late,
Such patience is displayed.
So lucky is me
To have the treat
Of a friend with whom to play.

It's not that I lack awareness of the ways of
the world, it's that I choose not to accept
them.

Bare Necessities
(Phones Are)

Need a new phone?
Of course.
It is essential now,
Between these two shores.
From sea to sea,
We need these things—
Oracle doors.
Knowledge of us stored;
Saved.
To us, they are engraved.
Maintained or replaced—
It's all the same.
All part of the game.

Tapioca Pearls

It's hard.
Too much to speak on,

About something so new

(To me.)

To me, it's a tradition,
Of which I haven't got a clue.

But as a fad, I was so glad for my diet to
include
Drink candy.

It's plain to see
This is my second favorite food (behind
spaghetti.)

Lavender liquid with beads soaked in honey
has
Saved me several times
From sadness.

It is a fad, yes?
But to me they're borderline divine.

Part of acceptance
Is loving new things, yes?

Changing intakes over time.

M.F.F.(H.)

Feminine gear includes
But is not limited to:
Bobby pins,
Bows,
Bras, and
Perfume.

Some may rather rock a baggy t-shirt, and
thin shoes.
Either way, it's safe to say,
Fashion is a tool one freely may choose.

When wearing outside,
A choice that is mine
Is a hairpiece of floral use;

About three inches of stem
Tucked into the hem
Of an ear for temporary use—
A stem chartreuse.

Well what I do find,
I tuck in behind,
And show off for all.
A bow phora—
My favorite flower (hibiscus.)

The Long Way

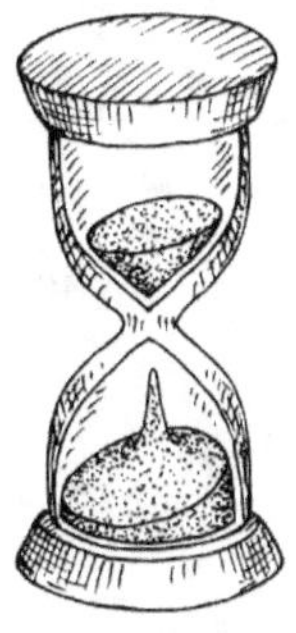

Not cheating
Takes more time.

If you play
With the way
You were intended to trudge through,
It may take you
An excruciatingly long time,
When judged by the ones who did it all
wrong.

For those who found shortcuts
By cutting others off—
Some may praise their quickly-paced cons.

You may be discouraged by your own path
when looking off.

Well how did they get there?

Guerilla warfare exists where

Shortcuts won't share

Victory built to last long.

Sometimes to take the way others will not

Is protection from people who refuse to play
along.

Pathy

Empathy is sharing wounds,
While sympathy is understanding you.

When confronted
Do not flee,
Simply ask
"Whose cruelty?"
When one is so keen
On destruction,
It is born
Of
Something.
To prevent future hurt,
Just learn.
We don't have to experience pain to
understand it—

Such synchronicity is overrated.
I can sympathize with you,
And who did it too.

Seeds

Area fifty-something is interesting;
The idea of interacting feels serene.
Who did all this testing?
Knowledge should be free.
For all that's holy—
Tell them, please.

Love is universal.

Feet Bare

It's scenic to wash feet
All sudsy,
Until they're squeaky clean,
After an outdoor journey.
So don't forget to scrub bark off
From the reading tree.
With Calypso tangerine
And steam means
Outside time is complete.
It's tough to touch grass
At least once a week.
It seems much more healthy
To keep
Feet bare.

It's essential for health
To breathe some fresh air.
Reading ten feet in the air
Is technically a climbing feat.
On some days, there's simply no place
That's better to be.

Scales for Feathers

Are they dragons?
How else could this happen?

Call up a halfling—
To save
Mountains of gold.

"What's all this work for?"

Those whose blood runs so cold.

Precious metals and gemstones
They behold.

And some said to the dwarves "Your enemies
are elves,"
So they fight among themselves
As the drakes hoard their wealth.

Scarcity, or Lack of Clarity?

There's no technology we lack
For all to be free and fed.

Charge for health?
Let me ask you
What's the cost of food,
And a warm bed?

Can we all simply seek that
Instead?

Creatures tall and small deserved to be fed.

What about surviving
Could keep them all from thriving,
Where there aren't so many heads?

Cast

Never broken a bone.
Everywhere is home.
Just selling some phones.
Leaning hard on loans.
Leaving no stone;
Not afraid of sticks or tones.
Can't we all just
Coexist?

DElulu

I'm delusional
For a world where we can be at peace,
Sitting on the porch together,
Sipping some tea.

Please forgive me
For wanting to see
What was in it for me.

Please forgive me
For being angry.
It's my response
To revealing these memories
Of family,
And never giving into feelings
That aren't set free.

We aren't made mean,
Just focused on menial things.
Please surrender to grit.

Juicy Bouquet

A random seed planted
In a place where flowers grow.

What started were leaves.
What would it become?

Instead of stems it grew a trunk;
Sturdy, brown, and lined with bark.

Fruit is born from flora;
Growing food for thought.

When another spring came
The whole tree
Blossomed.

Thirsty tree—
Queen of the garden.

Wireless Chargers

Lived through much,
Hurt a bunch,
And what I've learned
Is that some feed;
When you're angry
They're full and free.
So don't be.
Give them love, and feed them light.
You can't hurt me—
I'm quite alright.
That's what you have to say
To have a nice day.

Myself and I

There's two of me—
Through the same eyes, they see.

But what could set me free
If not my own key?

There's the me when I'm angry,
And the me when I'm free.

There's the me that loves me
Unconditionally.

So, which one am I gonna be today?

Free, or cave to hate?

Release, or relapse?

Let it go,
Or let it show?

A me I'm gonna be today is happy,
Because I know that peace is priceless.

I'm a princess—
My castle is home.

I couldn't think of a better place to go
Than home.

We made it together;
Family.

Mats

Humans are designed
To have a nap time;
Through the hottest part of the day,
And the coldest stretch of night.

Sugar and caffeine
Are such a false high.

Sleep will fulfill you
A million more times.

Hammocks are in the afternoon.
Cots are for the night.

Evenings are wide awake,
And so's the morning time.

Maybe one long rest is great,
Maybe that is fine.

Have you ever tried to sleep
Nap to nap, aligned?

Nice

Whichever way you now will steer,
(Whether planned or on a whim)
Hopefully our thoughts may meet—
What a journey it has been.

Through meadows, cups, and donut trips,
Through the past and present since,
Each line that's been brought to this point—
The future it will rinse.

And if I have but one request,
(Though some of it was dim)
Please hold on to all the best—
And wash away the grim.

Thank you for your time, my dear.
Thank you for the win.

www.ingramcontent.com/pod-product-compliance
Lightning Source LLC
Chambersburg PA
CBHW071331140726
47996CB00005B/1927